STAR BIOGRAPHIES

MEGHAN MARKLE

KENNY ABDO

Fly!
An Imprint of Abdo Zoom
abdobooks.com

abdobooks.com

Published by Abdo Zoom, a division of ABDO, P.O. Box 398166, Minneapolis,
Minnesota 55439. Copyright © 2019 by Abdo Consulting Group, Inc. International
copyrights reserved in all countries. No part of this book may be reproduced in any
form without written permission from the publisher. Fly!™ is a trademark and logo
of Abdo Zoom.

Printed in the United States of America, North Mankato, Minnesota.
092018
012019

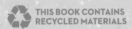

Photo Credits: Alamy, AP Images, Everette Collection, Getty Images, newscom,
Shutterstock, ©David Fisher p14 /Shutterstock, ©Vickie Flores p16/EPA-EFE/
Shutterstock
Production Contributors: Kenny Abdo, Jennie Forsberg, Grace Hansen
Design Contributors: Dorothy Toth, Neil Klinepier

Library of Congress Control Number: 2018946308

Publisher's Cataloging-in-Publication Data

Names: Abdo, Kenny, author.
Title: Meghan Markle / by Kenny Abdo.
Description: Minneapolis, Minnesota : Abdo Zoom, 2019 | Series: Star biographies
    | Includes online resources and index.
Identifiers: ISBN 9781532125461 (lib. bdg.) | ISBN 9781641856911 (pbk) |
    ISBN 9781532126482 (ebook) | ISBN 9781532126994 (Read-to-me ebook)
Subjects: LCSH: Meghan, Duchess of Sussex, 1981- (Rachel Meghan Markle)—
    Juvenile literature. | Princesses--Great Britain--Biography--Juvenile
    literature. | Television actors and actresses--Biography--Juvenile literature. |
    Harry, Prince, Duke of Sussex, 1984--Juvenile literature.
Classification: DDC 941.086092 [B]--dc23

TABLE OF CONTENTS

MEGHAN MARKLE

From the Hollywood Hills to Buckingham Palace, Meghan Markle has traveled a long road to royalty.

With a **resume** that includes actress, model, and calligrapher, she can now add **Duchess** of Sussex to the list!

EARLY YEARS

Rachel Meghan Markle was born in Los Angeles, California, in 1981.

Oregon

Idaho

Nevada

Utah

CALIFORNIA

Arizona

LOS ANGELES

She grew up in and around the entertainment business. After school, Markle would spend her time on set with her father. He was a lighting director for many TV shows.

Even at a young age, Markle was an outspoken feminist. At 11, she felt a commercial for Ivory Soap was sexist in its depiction of women. She wrote to the company and they changed the TV spot.

THE BIG TIME

After college, Markle began auditioning for acting **roles**. During that time, she would do **calligraphy** for weddings and events to make ends meet.

Markle also worked as a model and briefcase girl on the game show *Deal or No Deal* between auditions. She got her big break in the hit TV show *Suits* in 2011. She played one of the lead characters, Rachel, for seven seasons.

In 2016, Markle was set up on a **blind date** with Prince Harry. They married two years later. The ceremony was at the St. George's Chapel at Windsor Castle. She became Her Royal Highness the **Duchess** of Sussex.

Markle has retired from acting on screen. She now focuses on acting on behalf of the British Royal family.

LEGACY

Markle is the first American to marry into the British royal Family since 1936. She is also the first person to hold the title of **Duchess** of Sussex.

Markle was named one of the 100 most influential people in the world by TIME magazine in 2018. She was selected by Vogue magazine as one of the most influential women in the United Kingdom the same year.

GLOSSARY

blind date – a date with a person you have not met.

calligraphy – decorative handwritten lettering.

Duchess – the wife of a Duke.

resume – a short document that describes a person's work history.

role – a part an actor plays.

season – a set of episodes for a television series.

set – a place where a movie or a television show is recorded.

TV spot – another term for a television commercial.

ONLINE RESOURCES

Booklinks
NONFICTION NETWORK
FREE! ONLINE NONFICTION RESOURCES

To learn more about Meghan Markle, please visit abdobooklinks.com. These links are routinely monitored and updated to provide the most current information available.

INDEX